Community

Community

STARTING WELL IN YOUR SMALL GROUP

CONVERSATION GUIDE

EIGHT SESSIONS

ANDY STANLEY
AND THE NORTH POINT GROUPS TEAM

ZONDERVAN®
.com

NP
NORTH POINT
RESOURCES

ZONDERVAN

Community Conversation Guide
Copyright © 2013 by North Point Ministries, Inc.

This title is also available as a Zondervan ebook. Visit www.zondervan.com/ebooks.

Requests for information should be addressed to:

Zondervan, *Grand Rapids, Michigan 49530*

ISBN 978-0-310-81626-3

15 16 17 18 RRD 20 19 18 17 16 15 14 13 12 11 10 9 8 7 6 5 4

TABLE OF CONTENTS

WELCOME

Whether you've been in a small group before or this is your first time, we hope the next eight weeks will be different than anything you've experienced. You may have joined this group because you wanted to study the Bible, or you may just want the opportunity to meet some new people. In *Community: Starting Well in Your Small Group*, you'll do both. You'll explore biblical truth while building relationships with others. That's because we believe that *spiritual growth happens in the context of healthy relationships.*

A big part of this study is getting to know the other people in your group and letting them get to know you. We hope that as you come together with the purpose of growing closer to God, you'll experience joy and laughter, make new memories, and support one another during life's rough patches. We want you to view the next eight weeks as an opportunity to grow closer to God and closer to the other people in your group.

Because life really is better connected.

HOW TO USE THIS STUDY

BEFORE EACH GROUP MEETING

- Read the session's Introduction and Weekly Reading sections.
- Answer the Discussion Questions.

DURING EACH GROUP MEETING

- Read the session's Weekly Reading aloud.
- Watch the 15- to 20-minute video segment.
- Have a conversation about your answers to the Discussion Questions.
- Read the Moving Forward section aloud. This section challenges you to apply what you've learned and sets up the topic for the next session.

RENEWING YOUR MIND

Each session contains a key Bible verse that you can memorize or meditate on during the time between sessions.

A TYPICAL GROUP MEETING

Group meetings consist of three elements:

- Sharing—unstructured time when you connect relationally and talk about what's going on in your lives
- Study/discussion—time you spend studying the Bible, a book, a video series, or a curriculum
- Prayer—time you spend sharing prayer requests and praying for one another

You can decide as a group how you want to work these three elements into your meetings, but a typical two-hour group meeting might consist of 30 minutes of sharing, 60 minutes of study and discussion, and 30 minutes of sharing prayer requests and praying.

LEADER RESOURCES

You will find an in-depth Leader Guide designed to help you better facilitate the group experience by visiting:

groupleaders.org/startingwell

Groupleaders.org is also a great place to find other resources to help you throughout your group experience.

Session 1

SHOW UP

INTRODUCTION

Community isn't just a nice option; it's a need—like food, water, and shelter.

God created in us a need for him and for other people. We're relational beings because he is a relational being. Our community with others becomes the real-world setting where we practice the love that relationship with God produces in us.

[
**HE USES OTHER PEOPLE TO GROW US,
AND HE USES US TO GROW OTHER PEOPLE.**
]

Over the next eight sessions, we'll explore the connection between relationship with God and community with other people. We'll talk about how the two are essential components of growing spiritually and living life to the full.

The central purpose of this study is for you to get to know one another so you can set a firm foundation for a great Community Group experience.

You'll spend three of the eight sessions just telling one another your stories. But before you do that, we'll spend a couple of sessions talking about why community is important, why your stories matter, and how to best tell your stories.

WEEKLY READING:
WHAT TO EXPECT FROM THE GROUP EXPERIENCE

Community can be challenging because it's organic—every Community Group is different. Each is made up of different people with different backgrounds and experiences. But the very thing that can make community challenging can also make it great. As we get involved in real people's lives, faith leaves the realm of religious information and becomes a vibrant part of life in the real world. Jesus didn't give us a specific system or program with which to grow in our relationship with him. He gave us each other. He gave us community.

Life is better connected because connected people go further, faster.

Though the need for community is universal, there's a difference between what every person needs and what every group will provide. All groups are not equal at delivering community because all relationships are not equal at providing it.

FOUR KINDS OF RELATIONSHIPS

Our relationships fall into one of four categories:

PUBLIC
Connections through outside influences like a shared taste in music or a love of the same sports team.

SOCIAL
First-impression relationships based on surface-level interactions—acquaintances but not necessarily friends.

PERSONAL
Closer connections forged through shared experiences and feelings—friends.

INTIMATE
Real and raw connections—inner-circle friends. These relationships happen through our most closely shared experiences and feelings.

13

Most small groups are comprised of social and personal relationships. The deepest community happens through personal and intimate relationships. We hope this group will provide you with deep community. Whether it does will be partly determined by factors outside your control, like personal chemistry among the group members.

But some things *are* under your control. We'd like for you to do three things:

1. Show up.

Make a commitment to be at group meetings. You can't form community with other people if you aren't around enough for them to get to know you.

2. Join in.

Take part in group discussions. Listen to what others have to say. Be part of the community you're trying to form.

3. Be real.

Let the people in this group know who you are. Be authentic and transparent. You don't have to reveal all your deepest, darkest secrets. But be open to the possibility that you may eventually form the kind of deep relationships in which you can share those secrets.

ONE THING IS CERTAIN:

God has a purpose for this group and for everyone in it.

It may be a good experience for you or it may be a great experience. It will definitely be a place of growth and ministry if you pay attention to what God is doing through your relationships with one another.

YOUR FIRST GROUP MEETING

During your first session, you'll meet socially to begin to get to know one another. It's a good idea to commit to coming to the meeting with an open mind. Pray that God will use the group to grow his relationship with you and the other members of the group.

> *And let us consider how we may spur one another on toward love and good deeds, not giving up meeting together, as some are in the habit of doing, but encouraging one another—and all the more as you see the Day approaching.*
> Hebrews 10:24-25

Strength lies in differences, not in similarities.

STEPHEN R. COVEY

Every human activity can be put at the service of the divine and of love.

We should all exercise our gift to build community.

JEAN VANIER

Session 2

PURSUE GOD

INTRODUCTION

We all have relationships that feel weird—they're awkward and uncomfortable.

We don't want them to be, but they are.

MAYBE you can't find a way to talk to an adolescent.

MAYBE you're not sure what your parents really think of you and you can't muster the nerve to ask them.

MAYBE you've felt yourself drifting away from a close friend.

or **MAYBE** you see potential for friendship in a new acquaintance, but that person is holding you at arm's length.

> **FOR A LOT OF PEOPLE, THEIR RELATIONSHIP WITH GOD IS WEIRD AND AWKWARD.**

He can feel distant and uncaring—maybe even angry or judgmental. People think of him as a surly old man, a disapproving parent, or a humorless scold.

You may believe in God, but still wonder what he wants from you.

Does he like you?

Is he aware of how stressful life is—how you hate your job or are stressed out about your mortgage or concerned about your health or can't even believe how much it still hurts that your mom is gone?

Does he even care?

What if God does care?

What if he *wants* a relationship with you?

What if he wants to interact with you in a way
that is honest and transparent—*intimate*?

What if he wants your life to be filled with joy and peace?

That's the kind of God we all hope and long for, right?

If that's how God is, it would not only change your spiritual
life, it would change the way you relate to other people.

IT WOULD CHANGE EVERYTHING.

WEEKLY READING:
INTIMACY WITH GOD

Boiled down to its simplest form, the entire Bible—Old and New Testaments—is a record of God's pursuit of intimate relationship with his creation. God made everything around us so that it would reflect his glory and creativity. He made us in his own image to do the same. And he gave us the freedom to choose to love him . . . or not.

In Luke 15, Jesus tells three stories[1] to illustrate God's radical and relentless love for people.

In the first one, a man who has a hundred sheep loses one of them. So he leaves the ninety-nine and goes looking for the one until he finally finds it. The man is so happy he calls his friends and family together to celebrate.

In the second story, a woman with ten coins loses one of them. She turns her house upside down looking until she finds the lost coin. Like the man with the sheep, she celebrates recovering the coin with friends and family.

In the most famous story, a rebellious young man asks his dad for his inheritance (even though his dad is still alive) and then sets off on his own because he's tired of living by his father's rules. The young man squanders his money, learning the hard way that people who are your friends because of what they can get from you tend to disappear when you run out of stuff to give. When the young man realizes how much he's messed things up, he swallows his pride and goes back to his father's house, fully expecting to be punished.

INSTEAD, HIS DAD THROWS A PARTY AND INVITES ALL OF THEIR FAMILY AND FRIENDS—HE'S JUST HAPPY THAT HIS SON HAS COME HOME.

What Jesus' stories tell us is that God doesn't only look down on the mass of humanity from afar and feel love. He knows us and loves us individually. He cares about us personally. When we're lost, he finds us and brings us home. When we run away, he doesn't write us off. He waits patiently for us to return, ready to forgive and accept us.

---

[1] Luke 15:1–32

WE RESIST GOD BECAUSE WE DON'T TRUST HIM.

What if I depend on God and he lets me down? What if he takes advantage of me? What if he doesn't really have my best interests at heart?

When we decide that we can't trust God's love for us, our relationship with him becomes religion, which is just a quest to find the right combination of belief and ritual to get God to do what we want him to do. Because religion isn't relational, it reinforces our sense that God is distant and judgmental.

That kind of non-relationship with God eventually makes us judgmental. It's no way to live. It's definitely not God's design.

> The most powerful relational dynamic in the world is trust.

When two people set aside their own agendas on behalf of each other, it creates an unbreakable bond of trust between them. Each knows that the other has his or her best interests at heart.

God has already demonstrated his trustworthiness. When he sent Jesus to die for our sins, he put our need for salvation ahead of his son's suffering. By serving us, he invited us to trust him enough to obey him.[2]

---

[2] Philippians 2:6–8

So how do we pursue life-changing trust in God? It requires two things:

TIME

You can't have a relationship with someone without spending time with that person—casual, unstructured time.

In the case of God, we spend time with him at church or when we serve in a ministry. But that's not enough. We also need to spend time with him privately—reading the Bible, praying, and worshiping him.

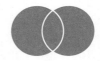

TRANSPARENCY

In our best relationships, we share all of ourselves, holding nothing back. In spite of our dark corners and hidden skeletons, we want to be fully known and accepted—loved—as we truly are.

Yet we're tempted to talk to God in formulas, using carefully selected words that brush over the messy parts of our lives so we don't offend him. It's easy to fall into this pattern. But don't be polite with God; be honest.

The spiritual life is a life in which you gradually learn to listen to a voice that says something else, that says, "You are the beloved and on you my favour rests."

HENRI J.M. NOUWEN

DISCUSSION QUESTIONS

1. What motivated you to join this group? What do you hope to get out of our time together?

2. On a scale of 1 to 10, with 1 being *"I'm not sure I believe in God"* and 10 being *"I spend time with God every day,"* where is your current relationship with God? (You can just give a number if you don't want to provide details.)

3. When you think about God, what do you imagine he is like?

4. What people or events in your life have influenced your picture of God?

5. What are some things that make it hard for people to trust God?

6. What is one thing you can do to give God more access to your life? What can this group do to support you?

MOVING FORWARD

Here's the thing: intimacy with God is the foundation for healthy relationships with other people. When we learn to trust God, he is able to grow our faith in surprising ways. That kind of relationship with God frees us to love others unconditionally instead of looking for something from them or trying to figure out how we can use them to get what we want.

We'll talk more about that in the next session.

> For I am convinced that neither death nor life, neither angels nor demons, neither the present nor the future, nor any powers, neither height nor depth, nor anything else in all creation, will be able to separate us from the love of God that is in Christ Jesus our Lord.
> **Romans 8:38–39**

To fall in love with God is the greatest of all romances; to seek him, the greatest

adventure; to find him, the greatest human achievement.

AUGUSTINE OF HIPPO

JOIN IN

Session 3

INTRODUCTION

We all put on acts.

We try to convince everyone that we have it all together:
- successful careers;
- strong, satisfying marriages;
- well-behaved children;
- crystal-clear consciences.

We go to extremes to create and protect the fake versions of ourselves that we present to the world. We buy cars and houses we can't afford. We suffer unsatisfying careers that happen to pay the bills. We hide our marital struggles instead of seeking help.

We keep secrets.

Have you ever had a raging argument in the car on the way to church with your spouse, children, boyfriend, or girlfriend, only to force smiles as you step into the building and make your way through the crowd? Most of us have.

> **BUT ISN'T THERE SOMETHING IN YOU—SOMETHING IN EACH OF US—THAT MAKES YOU WANT TO BE KNOWN FOR WHO YOU REALLY ARE?**

When we present false images to the people around us, we feel T E N S I O N. We feel like phonies, hypocrites. And at the deepest level, we know that's no way to live. We long for who we are in public to be the same as who we are behind closed doors.

A life in which there's only one version of us, no matter who we're around, sounds simple, pure, and magnetically attractive.

But it also feels unattainable. Even if we want to shed our false selves, there's a sense that a certain level of hypocrisy is part of being polite. We're not just fake because we want to look good. We're fake because we believe that no one really wants to hear our problems or deal with the ugly parts of our lives.

But what if there was a way to put aside the false images and just be you?

WEEKLY READING:
COMMUNITY WITH INSIDERS

Jesus designed Christian community to be the place we find wholeness, a congruency between who we are in public and who we are in private. He wants us to live together honestly and transparently. Not so we can be resigned to our brokenness, but so that we can begin to grow out of it, becoming more and more like him.

Jesus wants us to live abundantly. In John 10:10, he says, *"The thief comes only to steal and kill and destroy; I have come that they may have life, and have it to the full."* He didn't come to take from us or to harm us. He came to release us from sin so we could connect with God and to show us how to live meaningfully in community with one another. A full, free life begins with a trusting relationship with God and expands outward into trusting relationships with other people.

Scripture describes the kind of community Jesus wants us to build with one another:

Accept one another, then, just as Christ accepted you, in order to bring praise to God.
Romans 15:7

Accept the one whose faith is weak, without quarreling over disputable matters.
Romans 14:1

Carry each other's burdens, and in this way you will fulfill the law of Christ. If anyone thinks they are something when they are not, they deceive themselves.
Galatians 6:2–3

And let us consider how we may spur one another on toward love and good deeds.
Hebrews 10:24

Therefore confess your sins to each other and pray for each other so that you may be healed. The prayer of a righteous person is powerful and effective.
James 5:16

These passages describe a community that is inclusive, accepting those who are exploring faith, not treating them as though they have to figure everything out and clean up their lives before they're invited inside. It's a community in which people can be themselves and depend on one another. It's a community in which we don't stand in judgment of one another's flaws, but call one another to become our better selves—people who love and give to others.

Just like our relationship with God, our relationships with one another must be built on trust. And the ingredients for that trust are time and transparency.

TIME

To build the kind of community we desire for you, you'll need to spend time together—some of it structured around growing in your relationship with God and some of it casual and unstructured. Sometimes you need to just hang out with no agenda other than enjoying the company.

TRANSPARENCY

In Christian community, we share ourselves. Maybe not all the time and maybe not all at once, but this is the goal: to be real in every relationship and to actively build a few relationships in which nothing is held back.

We all struggle with sin and its effects. Bringing our struggles out into the light is the only way we become free from them. We do that by allowing ourselves to truly know and be known by others.

The idea of trusting other people with our true selves is scary because they might reject or condemn us. But think about it: if someone in this room opened up to you, would you reject or condemn him or her or would you offer support and be more inclined to be honest about who you are in return? If you'd respond with compassion, why assume the worst about others?

DISCUSSION QUESTIONS

1. Who was your best friend in childhood? What was it about that person that caused you to connect with him or her?

2. In what ways do people present exaggerated images of themselves to the world? What harm can these exaggerations cause?

3. Have you ever judged someone based on a first impression only to change your mind when you heard more of that person's story? What was it about hearing his or her story that changed your mind?

4. How do you feel about telling your story in this group?

5. If you were open and transparent in telling your story, how do you think it might change your relationships with the people in this group?

6. What are some things that could make this group safe enough for you to be open and transparent?

MOVING FORWARD

Trusting other people requires us to be honest with ourselves about who we are and to be bold enough to talk about it. That's not easy. But the goal of this community you're beginning to form is to grow to trust one another in ways outside your normal comfort zones. That won't happen overnight. It won't even happen by the time you're finished with this eight-week study. But it *can* happen and it begins with getting to know one another.

Over the next few sessions, you'll tell your stories. Before you end this session, spend some time setting up a schedule so everyone knows during which session he or she will be sharing. Depending on the size and makeup of your group, arrange for two or three individuals or couples to tell their stories each week (if you're a group of married couples, spouses should tell their stories together). Your leader or leaders will go first next session. One or two others should share as well.

> *And let us consider how we may spur one another on toward love and good deeds.*
> Hebrews 10:24

It is God's love for us that He not only gives us His Word but lends us His ear.

So it is His work that we do for our brother when we learn to listen to him.

DIETRICH BONHOEFFER

Sessi⬡ns 4-6

BE REAL

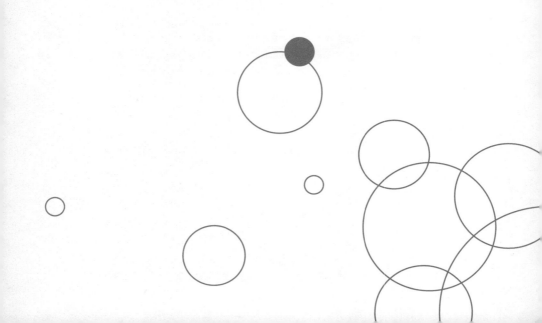

INTRODUCTION

Over the next few weeks, each of you will tell your story.

You may be eager to let others know who you are …

or you may be filled with anxiety.

Either way, use the information and exercises in this section to help you prepare.

THE MEMBERS OF YOUR GROUP HAVE CHOSEN TO BE IN COMMUNITY—a kind of community different from the teams, work environments, and casual friendships we normally experience.

Like you, they're looking for a community that spurs them into growth and a meaningful relationship with God and others. *Challenge yourself to be open and transparent. Let these people know who you really are.*

WEEKLY READING:
THE FIVE THINGS

When people tell their faith stories, five things appear over and over again—five things God uses to grow our faith. They're ways of recognizing how God is already involved in each of our lives. It's a great way for you to think through your own story.

PRACTICAL TEACHING

Studying the Bible and listening to sermons make Scripture seem alive and relevant in our daily lives. They show us who God is, who we are, and who God wants us to be.

PROVIDENTIAL RELATIONSHIPS

God uses the people in our lives to influence us in extraordinary ways. He speaks to us through others— whether lifelong friends or short-term acquaintances. Even difficult relationships can be used by God for our good.

PRIVATE DISCIPLINES

Things like prayer, personal time reading the Bible, fasting, and solitude deepen our relationship with God. They get our hearts in sync with his.

PERSONAL MINISTRY

Jesus showed us that we find life by giving our lives away. When we serve others, we are privileged to partner with God in what he's doing in the lives of those we serve.

PIVOTAL CIRCUMSTANCES

When big things happen, good or bad, they change the way we interact with God. Circumstances often cause us to pay attention to what he's doing in our lives.

> As you think about your own story, consider how the five things have played a part in your journey with God.

You don't have to talk about all five things, but maybe you've had a providential relationship or two that were crucial to growing your faith. Or maybe a pivotal circumstance revealed God's presence in your life. Or maybe a mission trip or other form of personal ministry changed your relationship with God. Very often, these five things represent changes in direction, challenges overcome, or life-changing revelations—things that make for interesting stories.

In a good story, a character wants something and overcomes obstacles to get it. When you think about it, your life's like that too. Whether you are looking for the perfect job, trying to get into the right school, or even falling in love, your story is probably about working for things you think will make you happy or give you a sense of purpose and meaning.

As you think about telling your story, consider the things you've wanted—career, family, adventure, spiritual experiences— and the obstacles you've faced while pursuing them.

BUT REMEMBER: The goal of your story isn't to entertain. It's not to be dramatic or funny (though it may be both). It's to share with your group the events and experiences that have helped to make you who you are.

MOVING FORWARD

As you think through your story, it may be helpful to ask the following questions:

> • *Who are the people who have most influenced me?*

> • *What are my greatest successes? What obstacles did I overcome to achieve those successes?*

> • *What are my greatest failures? What did I learn from those failures?*

> • *In what ways has God influenced my relationships, successes, and failures?*

If it helps, use the blank pages that follow to write notes, an outline, or a rough draft of your story. Keep in mind, though, that your story doesn't have to be polished and perfect. The most important thing is that it expresses who you are.

Reminder: Throughout Sessions 4-6, each member of your small group will be sharing their story, so please allow enough time for their stories to be told. During Sessions 5 and 6 there will be no video segments to watch in order to allow each member the time they need to tell their story.

> *I praise you for remembering me in everything and for holding to the traditions just as I passed them on to you.*
> 1 Corinthians 11:2

We get one story, you and I, and one story alone.

God has established the elements, the setting, and the climax and the resolution.

It would be a crime not to venture out, wouldn't it?

DONALD MILLER

Sitting around the table telling stories is not just a way of passing time.

It is the way the wisdom gets passed along. The stuff that helps us

to live a life worth remembering.

RACHEL NAOMI REMEN

Stories are the creative conversion of life itself into a more powerful, clearer,

more meaningful experience. They are the currency of human contact.

ROBERT MCKEE

Be yourself; everyone else is already taken.

OSCAR WILDE

Sessi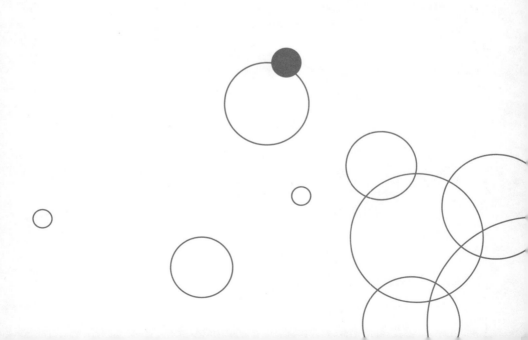n 7

BE THE CHURCH

INTRODUCTION

Over the past few sessions, you've told your stories.

You're getting to know each other beyond the surface details of jobs and hometowns and where you went to school. **NOW WHAT?** For the most part, you need to keep doing what you're doing. Building trust is an ongoing process.

In the weeks and months to come, you will

- read and talk about the Bible together,
- pray with and for one another,
- and just hang out.

[
BUT THERE'S SOMETHING ELSE YOU NEED TO DO:
INVEST IN THE LIVES OF OTHERS.
]

Christian community is designed to be outwardly focused, concerned with those who don't know Jesus, as well as those on the margins of society.[1] We have a responsibility to *express to the unloved and even the seemingly unlovable* the **GRACE AND MERCY** that we receive from God.[2]

[1] Luke 9:48
[2] Matthew 25:35–40

WEEKLY READING:
INFLUENCE WITH OUTSIDERS

Just before his crucifixion, Jesus prepared his disciples for his death. He began to show and tell them what they would need to do to establish his church and transform the world. During his last meal with them, he did something remarkable:

_____

It was just before the Passover Festival. Jesus knew that the hour had come for him to leave this world and go to the Father. Having loved his own who were in the world, he loved them to the end.

The evening meal was in progress, and the devil had already prompted Judas, the son of Simon Iscariot, to betray Jesus. Jesus knew that the Father had put all things under his power, and that he had come from God and was returning to God; so he got up from the meal, took off his outer clothing, and wrapped a towel around his waist. After that, he poured water into a basin and began to wash his disciples' feet, drying them with the towel that was wrapped around him.

He came to Simon Peter, who said to him, "Lord, are you going to wash my feet?"

Jesus replied, "You do not realize now what I am doing, but later you will understand."

"No," said Peter, "you shall never wash my feet."

Jesus answered, "Unless I wash you, you have no part with me."

"Then, Lord," Simon Peter replied, "not just my feet but my hands and my head as well!"

Jesus answered, "Those who have had a bath need only to wash their feet; their whole body is clean. And you are clean, though not every one of you." For he knew who was going to betray him, and that was why he said not every one was clean.

When he had finished washing their feet, he put on his clothes and returned to his place. "Do you understand what I have done for you?" he asked them. "You call me 'Teacher' and 'Lord,' and rightly so, for that is what I am. Now that I, your Lord and Teacher, have washed your feet, you also should wash one another's feet. I have set you an example that you should do as I have done for you. Very truly I tell you, no servant is greater than his master, nor is a messenger greater than the one who sent him. Now that you know these things, you will be blessed if you do them."
(John 13:1–18)

By washing his disciples' feet, Jesus inaugurated the kind of community he wanted us to live: one in which we overturn the natural order of the world by tenaciously putting others ahead of ourselves.

Jesus' radical act of service was an invitation to all of his followers—all of us—to participate with him in the transformation of people's lives. It's important that we prioritize relationships with unbelieving friends so that they can experience God's love the way we do. The easiest way to build influence with outsiders is to invest in the lives of unbelieving friends and, at the appropriate time, invite them to environments where they can hear spiritual truth. This isn't about selling someone on the idea of going to church. It's about reaching out and getting involved in people's lives so that they know the invitation is motivated by a genuine concern for them and that they're not just a project for you.

Another way to invest in the lives of people around us is to serve those in need. Jesus' call for us to serve others can make us uncomfortable. It's easier to do nothing. We're tempted to view poverty and sickness and human suffering as too large for us to make much of a difference. But Jesus didn't call you to live in a cloistered community that holds outsiders at bay. He'll take responsibility for changing the world, but he wants you to be involved in his work. It's true that you can't serve everyone in need, but you can serve someone in need.

And this small community that you're in the process of forming will benefit enormously from investing in the lives of the people around you—whether it's investing in and praying for unbelieving friends or serving those in need. That time spent doing something important together will draw you into greater transparency. It will increase your trust—*of God and of one another.*

Only a life lived for others is a life worthwhile.

ALBERT EINSTEIN

DISCUSSION QUESTIONS

1. Talk about a time when you got to see people in a new context (for example, going out to dinner with coworkers). How did that experience change the relationships in that group?

2. How do you think doing something together outside of group meetings could change the relationships in this group?

3. What is the connection between investing in others and growing in your relationship with God? Why do you think God set things up that way?

4. How could serving others change people's perceptions of Christians and the church?

5. What kinds of things keep us from investing in or serving others?

6. Is there a charity or a particular group in need that is near and dear to your heart? If so, talk about why you feel a desire to help that charity or group.

MOVING FORWARD

Individually, think about an unbelieving friend, neighbor, or coworker whose life you can begin to invest in so that when the time is right you can invite him or her to church. What is the best next step for you to take with that person?

As a group, begin planning to serve with one another. Talk about it. Do any of you feel a burden to serve a particular group of people in need—single moms, children living in poverty, AIDS patients, shut-ins? If so, this may help you figure out where you can serve. But the important thing is to serve someone. Once you start serving, do so on a regular basis—monthly, quarterly, whatever you decide as a group.

Don't move beyond the planning phase until you've committed to move forward with your group. That will happen next session. But once you've committed to moving forward, get out and serve some people as soon as you can. If you don't serve within the first few months you're together, time will fly by and you may miss the opportunity entirely.

The **HOW DO WE SERVE?** section in this guide will help you generate ideas and set up a service opportunity.

> *You, my brothers and sisters, were called to be free. But do not use your freedom to indulge the flesh; rather, serve one another humbly in love. For the entire law is fulfilled in keeping this one command: "Love your neighbor as yourself."*
> Galatians 5:13–14

Everybody can be great . . . because anybody can serve. You don't have to have a

college degree to serve. You don't have to make your subject and verb agree to serve.

You only need a heart full of grace. A soul generated by love.

MARTIN LUTHER KING, JR.

HOW DO WE SERVE?

NEED HELP CONNECTING WITH SOMEONE IN NEED?

- Ask a friend who works in healthcare.
- Check with your leasing office or a counselor at your child's school.
- Contact a local government group, like the Parks and Recreation Department.
- Call a well-connected neighbor or coworker.

YOUR SERVICE OPPORTUNITY STEP-BY-STEP

1. Consult your calendars, save a Saturday, and psyche yourselves up to serve.
2. Kick off your service day by gathering for breakfast at a restaurant or one of your homes.
3. Take pictures while you serve. Use one as the wallpaper on your computer or phone.

SERVICE IDEAS

- Organize a cell phone or eyeglass drive.

- Rake leaves, clean gutters, or power wash a driveway for a neighbor in need.

- Assemble a new parent's kit for the arrival of a newborn and then donate the kit to a crisis pregnancy center.

- Throw a "PB&J" party. Bring supplies to your small group gathering and make peanut butter and jelly sandwiches. Donate the sandwiches to a nearby shelter or food pantry.

- Identify a school playground or local park that could use some sprucing up. Plan a day of painting, raking, and mulching.

- Throw a cookie-decorating party, manicure party, or Christmas sing-along at a nursing home.

- Put together care packages for soldiers. You can find organizations online that will help with mailing and provide wish-list items to send.

- Renovate used or broken furniture and then deliver it to a needy family or donate it to a nonprofit.

- Choose an easy craft you can do as a group, like making fleece blankets. Then donate your work to a hospital.

- Adopt a family at Christmas by purchasing gifts for the children.

- Sell hot coffee or warm doughnuts in your neighborhood and then donate your earnings to a nonprofit.

- Clip coupons from the Sunday paper, go grocery shopping, and donate the food to a local shelter or pantry.

Sessi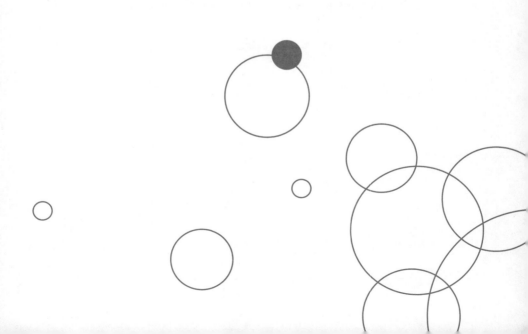n 8

BE TOGETHER

INTRODUCTION

Over the past seven sessions, you've learned that spiritual growth is evidenced by intimacy with God, community with insiders, and influence with outsiders.

You've also invested time sharing your stories and getting to know one another.

[
NOW IS THE TIME TO COMMIT TO CONTINUING AS A GROUP.
]

In this final session, we'll review the values and goals in the **COMMUNITY GROUP AGREEMENT.** As a group, you'll work out the logistics of group meetings moving forward. This simple exercise is a great way to ensure that everyone's expectations are aligned.

If you decide not to move forward with your group, contact your leader by phone or email before the next meeting to let him or her know. If this group isn't a fit for you, don't worry about it. And don't give up on the idea of community.

All groups are different; there's one out there for you.

WEEKLY READING:
COMMUNITY GROUP VALUES AND GOALS

A Community Group should provide a predictable environment where group members can pursue healthy relationships and spiritual growth.

Relationships
While prayer and discussion of curriculum are key elements, the driving force behind the group is the building of relationships.

Authenticity
The atmosphere should encourage openness and transparency among members. This is an environment where people should feel free to be themselves.

Confidentiality
For authenticity to occur, members must be able to trust that issues discussed within the group will not be shared outside the group.

Respect
Group members should never say anything that will embarrass their spouses or other members of the group.

Availability
A primary responsibility of the group is to prioritize specific relationships. This requires a willingness to be available to meet one another's needs.

Multiplication
Group members recognize that one of the goals of their group is to start a new group within the life cycle of the group. This allows others to experience the Community Group relationship.

MOVING FORWARD

Congratulations on finishing *Community: Starting Well in Your Small Group*. We hope that you've had a chance to get to know the other people in your group and to let them get to know you. We hope you've experienced the truth that *life really is better connected.*

We recommend that you make your next group meeting a social. Take a little time to just hang out and celebrate what you've experienced together over the past couple of months. Use some of the time to decide what you'll study next as a group.

> *"A new command I give you: Love one another. As I have loved you, so you must love one another. By this everyone will know that you are my disciples, if you love one another."*
> John 13:34–35

The world is so empty if one thinks only of mountains, rivers and cities; but to know someone who thinks and feels with us, and who, though distant, is close to us in spirit, this makes the earth for us an inhabited garden.

JOHANN WOLFGANG VON GOETHE

Our lives are connected by a thousand invisible threads.

HERMAN MELVILLE

Christian DVD Study

It's Not What You Think

Andy Stanley

According to Andy Stanley, the words used to describe Christians today often bear no resemblance to what Jesus wanted his followers to be known for.

In this eight-session video study (participant's guide sold separately), you'll learn:

- What one word should be descriptive of every Christian
- How Jesus' followers should treat those who are outside the faith
- Why people love Jesus but can't stand his followers

What does is mean to be Christian? Curiously, the term is never used in Scripture. Instead, Christian was a label used by outsiders to define Jesus' followers. Jesus referenced "disciple" as the key word he used to describe his supporters along with the fact that they would be known for their love—a novel concept for their time—and ours today.

Sessions include:

1. Brand Recognition
2. Quitters
3. Insiders, Outsiders
4. Showing Up
5. When Gracie Met Truthy
6. Angry Birds
7. Loopholes
8. Working It Out

Guardrails DVD Study
Avoiding Regrets in Your Life

Andy Stanley

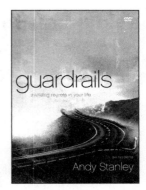

[Guardrails: a system designed to keep vehicles from straying into dangerous or off-limit areas.]

They're everywhere, but they don't really get much attention . . . until somebody hits one. And then, more often than not, it is a lifesaver.

Ever wonder what it would be like to have guardrails in other areas of your life—areas where culture baits you to the edge of disaster and then chastises you when you step across the line?

Your friendships. Your finances. Your marriage. Maybe your greatest regret could have been avoided if you had established guardrails.

In this six-session video based study (participant's guide sold separately), Andy Stanley challenges us to stop flirting with disaster and establish some personal guardrails.

Session titles:

1. Direct and Protect
2. Why Can't We Be Friends
3. Flee Baby Flee!
4. Me and the Mrs.
5. The Consumption Assumption
6. Once and For All

Available in stores and online!

Taking Responsibility for Your Life DVD Study

Because Nobody Else Will

Andy Stanley

RESPONSIBILITIES. We all have them. But we don't all take them as seriously as we ought to. Wouldn't it be great, though, if we all took responsibility for the things we are responsible for? Wouldn't it be great if you took responsibility for everything you're responsible for? It's time to stop the finger-pointing and excuse-making and to remove the "ir" in irresponsible. In this four-part video series (participant's guide sold separately), Andy Stanley tells us it's time to ask ourselves, "Am I REALLY taking responsibility for my life?"

Session titles:

1. Let the Blames Begin
2. The Disproportionate Life
3. This Is No Time to Pray
4. Embracing Your Response Ability

Available in stores and online!

Five Things God Uses to Grow Your Faith DVD Study

Andy Stanley

Imagine how different your outlook on life would be if you had absolute confidence that God was with you. Imagine how differently you would respond to difficulties, temptations, and even good things if you knew with certainty that God was in all of it and was planning to leverage it for good. In other words, imagine what it would be like to have PERFECT faith. In this DVD study, Andy Stanley builds a biblical case for five things God uses to grow BIG faith.

In six video sessions, Andy covers the following topics:

- Big Faith
- Practical Teaching
- Providential Relationships
- Private Disciplines
- Personal Ministry
- Pivotal Circumstances

Along with the separate participant's guide, this resource will equip groups to become more mature followers of Jesus Christ.

How to Be Rich book with DVD

It's Not What You Have. It's What You Do with What You Have.

Andy Stanley

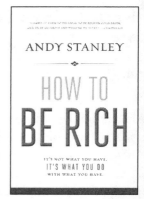

How to Be Rich: A DVD Study is a small group Bible study from pastor Andy Stanley exploring 1 Timothy 6:18. Andy biblically redefines what wealth is, how to use it, and helps you and your group practice being rich so you will be good at it if you should ever be so fortunate.

The early Christians took this command seriously. Generosity was the hallmark of the early church. They did for those who could not do or would not do anything in return. That was new. That got people's attention.

Is that how people in our communities would describe us?

This small group study is a tool that will force conversation and reflection around the topic of what to do with what we have. Jesus could not have been any clearer. It's not what you have that matters. It's what you do with what you have that will count for you or against you in the kingdom of heaven.

Andy will encourage you and your group to look at richness differently, which might just lead our families, communities, and world to looking at Christians differently. The pack contains *How to Be Rich: A DVD Study* and the *How to Be Rich* book, which includes small group discussion questions.

Zondervan Small Group Bible Study YouTube Playlist

Watch Over 100 Full Bible Study Sessions for Free

Watch the entire first session for many of Zondervan's video-based Bible studies. No more guessing on the content; instead you get the full video experience by being able to see and evaluate the complete first session of each multi-session Bible study.

Each video is easy to share with your friends, small group, or Bible study. Just hit the "share" button under the video and send it via email, Facebook, or Twitter.

Watch Bible study sessions from bestselling authors like Andy Stanley, Timothy Keller, Anne Graham Lotz , Bill Hybels, Craig Groeschel, Jim Cymbala, John Ortberg, Lysa TerKeurst , and many more.

Zondervan video-based group Bible studies are available on DVD, and many are available for download. These video Bible studies feature a variety of topics from many authors, and are available wherever small group resources and curriculum are sold.

Watch sessions from bestselling studies including:

* *Guardrails* by Andy Stanley
* *The Reason for God* by Timothy Keller
* *The Christian Atheist* by Craig Groeschel
* *Undaunted* by Christine Caine
* *The Circle Maker* by Mark Batterson

Available in stores and online!

Share Your Thoughts

With the Author: Your comments will be forwarded to the author when you send them to *zauthor@zondervan.com*.

With Zondervan: Submit your review of this book by writing to *zreview@zondervan.com*.

Free Online Resources at
www.zondervan.com

Daily Bible Verses and Devotions: Enrich your life with daily Bible verses or devotions that help you start every morning focused on God. Visit www.zondervan.com/newsletters.

Free Email Publications: Sign up for newsletters on Christian living, academic resources, church ministry, fiction, children's resources, and more. Visit www.zondervan.com/newsletters.

Zondervan Bible Search: Find and compare Bible passages in a variety of translations at www.zondervanbiblesearch.com.

Other Benefits: Register to receive online benefits like coupons and special offers, or to participate in research.